Walks w

SC....

LAKELAND

Dennis and Jan Kelsall

^A QUESTA Guide

© Dennis and Jan Kelsall, 2001, 2005
ISBN 1 898808 09 0

PUBLISHER'S NOTE
It is the responsibility of parents when out walking
with children to supervise them and to make
judgements about whether any part of a walk is
unsuitable for them.

Readers are advised that while the authors have made
every effort to ensure the accuracy of this
guidebook, changes can occur which may affect the
contents. The Publishers would welcome notes of any
changes you find.

Neither the authors nor Questa Publishing Limited can
accept responsibility for any inaccuracies, or for any
injuries or damage that may occur while following the
routes in this book.

Maps:
The maps accompanying the walks in this book are
reproduced by permission of Ordnance Survey on behalf
of HMSO. © Crown copyright, 2005. All rights reserved.
Ordnance Survey Licence number 100043743.

Also by Dennis and Jan Kelsall
Walks with Children in the Lake District:
Ambleside and Grasmere
Around Kendal
Around Windermere
Short Walks around the Eden Valley & North Pennines

Published by
Questa Publishing Limited, PO Box 520, Bamber Bridge, Preston,
Lancashire PR5 8LF
and printed by
Carnmor Print, 95/97 London Road, Preston, Lancashire PR1 4BA

Contents

Introduction

Overlooking the vast openness of Morecambe Bay, South Lakeland has a wonderfully scenic landscape. Yet much of it is relatively unfrequented, often passed through on the way to somewhere else, but rarely a destination for its own sake. This is at the same time both sad and fortunate. On the one hand, many people miss the opportunity to discover some of Lakeland's better kept secrets, but the advantage is that its paths are rarely crowded and often, you can almost have the place to yourselves.

Before the mid-nineteenth century, the area was relatively isolated from the rest of the country. The few roads that did exist, meandered for miles around the heads of the Kent and Leven estuaries and their poor condition made progress slow and difficult. As a consequence, many travellers arriving from the south chose the more direct route across the glistening sands from Hest Bank near Morecambe. The passage was known and used in antiquity, but the way has never been without danger. The river channels and sandbanks are constantly shifting and the incoming tide has been known to advance as a wall, at a speed faster than a man can run, and a hooter is still sounded at the turn of the tide to warn the unwary. Monks from Cartmel and Cornishead Priories once guided wayfarers across but, after the Dissolution, that duty was assumed by the Crown, a tradition that continues today in the form of the present Queen's guide, Cedric Robinson. There are stunning views across the estuary from several of the walks in this book and, although beyond the scope of these pages, the trek across the sands is an unforgettable experience, particularly for children. So if you ever get the chance, join one of Cedric's crossings.

The extension of the railway from Carnforth around the coast to Barrow in 1857 immediately brought the area in reach of Lancashire's industrial towns and the developing holiday resorts of Blackpool and Morecambe – the tourist age had begun. On the coast, Grange grew as a genteel resort and day-trippers took excursions into the hinterland to enjoy its picturesque scenery. Trains to Lakeside connected with boats sailing the length of Windermere to Ambleside and some passengers even continued by coach to Coniston before returning to Fleetwood via Barrow by train and ferry, all for the princely sum of 7/6d (37½p). Many youngsters, as well as the not so young, will be delighted to know that trains again run between Haverthwaite (where one of our walks begins) and Lakeside, and a steam boat still plies the lake to Ambleside. You can also make use of the regular coastal rail service to reach Grange, whose station is close to the start of one of the walks to the top of Hampsfell.

But in exploring this fascinating area, you will not just be following in the footsteps of Victorian holidaymakers, for it was once a place of much industry too. Until the founding of the monastic houses in the eleventh century, the predominant activity in the region had been farming, but the monks found other sources of wealth in rich mineral deposits, and it was they who first managed the forests, harvesting the trees to provide a steady source of wood for charcoal burning and timber for building and other uses. The charcoal was used to heat small foundries and forges for the production and working of iron, and remains of these industries are still to be found amongst the trees. Charcoal was also used to make gunpowder, much in demand by the many quarries around the area. Two of our walks pass by former gunpowder factories, near Sizergh and at Low Wood near Haverthwaite. The fast flowing streams were exploited to provide power and dozens of mills were built to serve a host of different purposes. Several of our walks pass by such sites, but the only one still working is at Stott Park Bobbin Mill, near the beginning of the Thwaite Head route.

Throughout the medieval period, the area's largest town, Kendal was an important trade and manufacturing centre, with wool and woven goods being the major commodities. However, as the industrial age began, Kendal found itself too remote to retain its importance and in an attempt to remedy this, the Lancaster Canal was begun. It was planned to run from Kendal to Liverpool, crossing the Ribble valley on an aqueduct at Preston and joining the Leeds Liverpool Canal near Chorley. The aqueduct was never built, but at Hincaster, just south of Kendal, a tunnel was dug right through the hill, to avoid an otherwise lengthy detour. Although many sections of the canal have now disappeared, some of it beneath the M6 motorway, Hincaster Tunnel remains, and makes a fascinating objective for another of our walks.

In the event, Kendal and Lakeland beyond were thankfully spared from most of the horrors of the new industrial age, but the previously thriving cottage-type industries were unable to compete with mass production and so died out. Sheep farming continued, as did tourism, to become the main 'industries' of the area. However, tourist patterns have shifted considerably during the twentieth century, the age of the car symbolising unprecedented freedom and mobility, and bringing the very heart of the high mountains in reach of the Sunday afternoon driver. The stark peaks have lost the awe and terror imagined by Victorian travellers and, for those intent on something more than traipsing around Bowness' glitzy shops, it is these high points that are now often the main attraction. Yet, Lakeland has many other facets too, and it is some of these that are explored here.

Which brings us back more or less to where we began. The area covered in this book offers some wonderful walking in beautiful countryside. The diversity of paths and tracks threading through it all create hundreds of opportunities for individual exploration, in a way that the, by now, well-worn mountain routes can no longer satisfy. True, there are some popular routes included here, but that is because they really have something special to offer, in their views and the countryside passed. Whilst there is nothing overly strenuous, which makes them an ideal introduction for younger members of the family to the delights of walking and countryside exploration, each offers a sense of achievement, which will hope-fully encourage a lifelong pleasure in countryside walking.

The wealth of historical background and variety of wildlife habi-tats mean that there is always something to look out for and encourage enquiring minds. It is a good idea to take along a field guide to help identify some of the many birds, insects, flowers and trees you will come across. You may see some of the area's animals too, such as deer, foxes, hares plus other smaller crea-tures as well. Although few of these walks attain any great height, the generally open nature of the surrounding countryside allows some quite spectacular views. Indeed, on the top of Hampsfell you will find a wonderful observation post, complete with a sighting arm and a table of things to be seen. Children will love aligning the pointer on the distant peaks and it gives an insight as to how the first maps were made. But don't let them monopolise it too much, because grown-ups like to play with it as well!

1
The Hills behind Bowness

Although one of the longer walks in this collection, apart from a bit of a climb out of Bowness, there is nothing difficult or overly strenuous about it and it gives a most delightful ramble across the rolling pasture and gentle low fells that lie to the east of Windermere.

Total distance: 8.1 miles (13km)
Height gain: 1,150 feet (350m)
Start: St Martin's Parish Church in Bowness.
GR.403969

1   Leave the main road opposite Bowness Parish Church and walk up St Martin's Hill and then Brantfell Road, climbing steadily away from the town for about ¼ mile. The road ends at a gate, from which a footpath ascends the field ahead, passing a stone slab seat marking the beginning of the Dales Way. Leave the field at the top and turn right onto a crossing track leading into a wood. Where the track shortly bends sharply left, leave it and walk ahead through a kissing-gate onto Post Knott, a lovely National Trust viewpoint overlooking Windermere.

2   Now, with your back to the lake, walk across to a ladder-stile leading to open ground below Brant Fell. Climb, initially beside a fence on the left but then bear right along a faint grass path, marked by prominent cairns to reach the obvious summit.

3   After enjoying the view, return to the last cairn passed on the way up. There turn right and, following more cairns, walk down to a track at the base of the hill. Go right and walk to its end, emerging through a gate onto a lane.

4   Turn right and, at a cross-roads a short distance on, walk ahead along Lindeth Lane. After ½ mile, leave the lane along a drive on the left towards Low Lindeth Farm, signed as a footpath to Green Lane. However, at a waymark, 100 yards along, abandon the drive, and bear right along a faint track across the open heath. The route is occasionally

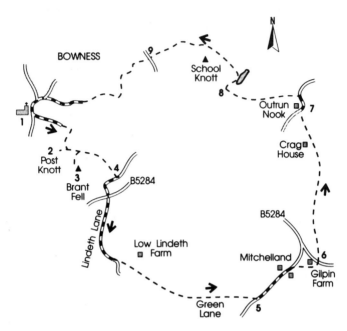

confirmed by waymarks and eventually leads to a ladder-stile over a lateral wall. Bear left away from the wall, a vague track maintains your direction, rising across the wilder heath beyond. The way is sometimes confused by crossing sheep tracks, but keep going and higher up, when a conspicuous cairn comes into view on the skyline, aim to the right of it. You will then shortly join a track, which to the right, leads out through a gate onto Green Lane. There, turn left and walk to its end.

5 Now back on a lane, turn left and follow it for about 1/3 mile until you reach some cottages at Mitchelland. Immediately after a cottage on the right, leave the lane for a marked footpath beside it, which crosses a stream into the corner of a field. Walk left, crossing a stile into a second field, towards Gilpin Farm. Immediately past the barns, turn right and then left through the farmyard, leaving along a metalled track. Bear left when it forks and climb up to the road at the top, the B5284.

6 The onward route lies directly opposite, along an enclosed climbing

grass track that leads to an open field at the top. Keep going, shortly passing through a second gate. A little way beyond that, where the main track bends right, leave it on a lesser path continuing ahead, shortly passing through a gate by a stream. Keep going in the same direction and, after cresting a rise, drop to cross the stream again and then another gate. Follow the stream up to a final gate, emerging onto a stone track below Crag House Farm. Go left, but where the track turns into the farm, bear right beside a wall and join another track leading away from the farm into a field. As you walk down, bear left beyond a rocky knoll, dropping through a gate onto a lane by Outrun Nook.

7   Turn right, but after about 200 yards, leave the lane along a track on the left marked as the Dales Way. Immediately after passing a cottage, turn right and walk through a gate beside a barn to the field beyond. A track leads beside a broken wall across a stile and then gently climbs the open hillside, shortly passing through a gap in a crossing wall. Not far past there, the track bends to the right and leads through another wall before dropping left to a gate in the bottom corner.

8   Through that, turn right, the way rising to pass a small tarn. Half-way along, turn left and climb to a kissing-gate. Beyond, a grassy trod leads you over the obvious high point, School Knott. Maintain your direction down the far side, passing through a kissing-gate towards the bottom. Lower down, bear left to reach a tarmac track and follow it left through a gate. After passing a cottage on the left, Old Droomer, turn right down stone steps and across a stream into a field. Walk away, initially with a wall on your right, but higher up, climbing beside a wall on the left to a stile in the top corner out to a lane.

9   Opposite to the right, is a kissing-gate, from which a green trod drops to pass behind houses. Beyond them, go through another kissing-gate and down a wooded bank to a crossing path at the bottom. Turn left, waymarked to Bowness, and walk around the back of more houses to a fork, where you should bear left and cross a stile. The onward path takes you through more gates, finally reaching a track, where you should turn right. Shortly becoming a road, it leads into the town and ends at the main road. St Martin's Church, from where you began the walk, lies at the bottom of the hill.

2

Satterthwaite and Rusland

For centuries, the forest here was an industrious place, with the smoke from charcoal burning and iron smelting hanging in the branches and the thud of forging hammers carrying through the trees. These industries have helped preserve the character and extent of the forest, which was extensively managed to provide a continuous and renewable supply of timber, rather than cleared for use as grazing land.

Total distance: 5.6 miles (9km)
Height gain: 885 feet (270m)
Start: Blind Lane forest car park, south-east of Satterthwaite. GR.345913

1   Follow a path at the rear of the car park, indicated by green and white markers, through the trees to the right, gently climbing north-east to reach a forest trail. There turn left, but after 450 yards, leave for a path on the left rising through a birch wood. At the top, cross directly over a forest trail and carry on along the continuation of the footpath. Keep to the main path as it loses height, eventually reaching cottages at Satterthwaite.

2   Beyond the first building, the way emerges onto a narrow metalled lane that, to the right, leads to a junction in the village by the church. There, turn left and follow the road away, past an inn and over a bridge. After ¼ mile, at a left-hand bend in the road, bear right onto a rough track that follows the edge of a wood. A short distance along, leave it at a green marker, going left on a path climbing into the trees.

* *Just before the crest of the hill, to the right is a small circular hut. It*
* *is part of the Grizedale art project and as you wander along the*
* *forest tracks, you will come across other strange and wonderful*
* *objects, so keep your eyes open.*

3   Beyond there, the path eventually descends to a forest track, where you should turn right.

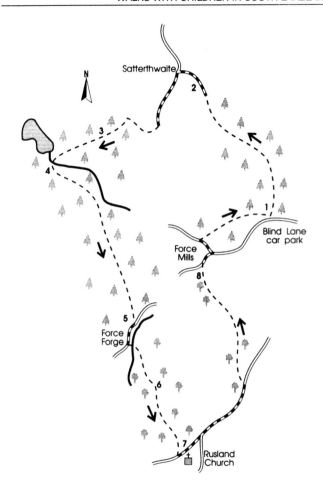

4   After crossing the stream, the track rises to a junction. Turn left and walk on as far as a fork, where a grass track leaves on the left. This descends along a lovely wooded valley below the main track, ending over a stile onto a lane – take care negotiating any trunks that may have fallen across the path.

5   Turn right along the lane 200 yards to a group of cottages and then go left at a waymark into a small courtyard between them. Over a gate/ stile on the right, carry on along a path beside a tall beech hedge, which leads behind the settlement to a bridge spanning Force Beck. On the other side, a winding path leads into a wood, shortly meeting a rough track where you should turn right. Follow this for about ¼ mile until, after levelling from a gradual climb, the track approaches a crossing wall. However, before you reach it, turn off onto a fainter path heading to a gap in the wall over to the left.

6   After crossing a stream on its far side, the path turns left, initially beside the wall and then later leaving it to pursue a winding descent through the trees. Lower down, bear right and drop to the side of a stone building, Rusland Parish Hall, where a wall-stile leads past it onto a lane opposite Rusland Church.

* *The graveyard of this tiny church is the resting place for the ashes*
* *of Arthur Ransome, the author of several books including the*
* *childrens stories of 'Swallows and Amazons'. He was born in Leeds*
* *in 1884, but developed a deep and lasting passion for the area when*
* *still a young boy, through annual family holidays he spent at High*
* *Nibthwaite on the banks of Coniston.*

7   From the Parish Hall, turn left to walk north-east along the lane to a road junction. There, an unmarked track on the left climbs through a gate, ahead along the edge of a hillside pasture. Towards the top, continue through another gate before gently descending the far side of the hill to the track's eventual end, where it emerges onto a lane at Force Mills.

* *The buildings here were also associated with the iron smelting and*
* *forging industries. Watermills harnessed the power of the swiftly*
* *flowing streams to operate bellows and a heavy forge hammer.*

8   Turn right, but then go left at a junction a few yards on, to climb beside Force Falls, they lie hidden in the trees over to the left. A little way up the hill, leave the lane for a woodland path rising on the right, indicated by green and white markers. Where it shortly forks, bear right, continuing to climb by a wall. Higher up, the path passes through the wall and then reaches another fork. There bear right again, recrossing the wall to descend through the trees, the path returning you to the car park at Blind Lane.

3
Thwaite Head

A longer walk combining woodland and forest with arresting views across open countryside and an opportunity to dabble by the shore of Windermere. Although there is a climb towards the end of the walk, the view that is revealed from the top of Stott Park Heights is quite enthralling and justifies a second picnic stop to savour it to the full.

Total distance: 9 miles (14.5km)
Height gain: 1,410 feet (430m)
Start: High Dam car park near Finsthwaite. GR.369881

1   From a gate by an information panel, follow a broad track from the car park into the woodland beyond. Take either branch at a fork, the paths rejoining higher up to pass through a second gate. Beyond that, bear left and continue past a small reservoir to the foot of a second, larger lake. Turn left across its retaining dam and follow the continuing footpath part-way around the western shore.

2   After leaving the lake, the path passes through a wall and turns left, signed to Rusland. At first follow a wall, but after a couple of stiles, carry on over a mossy heath, eventually descending an open hillside. As the ground falls, a splendid view over the Rusland valley opens up, set against a backdrop of the distant Coniston hills. Lower down, beyond a pair of stiles, walk ahead across a stream and then bear right descending on a winding field path, eventually to pass through a wall gap at the bottom. Keep going ahead, finally leaving the fields over a stream and through a gate/stile to follow a track.

3   Reaching a lane at the bottom, turn left to Crosslands, then at a junction beyond the cottages, go right to Satterthwaite. At Thwaite Head, ¾ mile away, cross a skew-arched bridge and then go right over a wooden foot-bridge, climbing between cottages to a junction. Turn left, but then immediately go right through a waymarked gate/stile into a field.

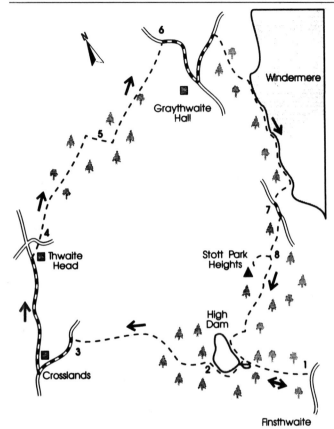

Finsthwaite

4   A grass track rises to a gate by its top corner and on into a wood. Keep ahead, initially between a wall and stream and, where the track later forks, follow the right-hand branch. After running by a marshy area the climb resumes, successively crossing a stile, a wall gap and then a second stile, eventually passing into forest. Then, bear right to reach a junction of paths 50 yards away and go right again, dropping over a stream to a couple of stiles immediately beyond. Over those, climb with the wall on your left, later recrossing it by a stile.

5   Reaching a forest road, go diagonally over to the right and follow the path's continuation alongside a wall and then through it, at a waymarked

break higher up. Walk directly away from the wall to join a forest track a short distance on. Go ahead, rising over the crest of a hill and down the far side, eventually reaching a junction. Turn left, but at the next junction, turn right onto a climbing track through the trees. Shortly passing into more open oak wood, the path peaks before falling between wood and forest to a track at the bottom. Go left, passing some cottages and then left again to leave Graythwaite Park onto a lane.

6   Walk right to a junction opposite Graythwaite Hall and turn left towards Cunsey and Sawrey Ferry. After about 600 yards, at a waymark, leave along a fenced woodland path on the right. Keep ahead over crossing tracks, eventually descending to Windermere, where you should turn right on a lakeside path. Continue beside the water's edge for ¾ mile until the path finally abandons the lake, returning through the wood to emerge onto a road.

7   Go left to the entrance of the YMCA centre and cross to a permissive path through a gate on the right, which climbs the steep, wooded hillside above the road to another gate. Through that, continue climbing, winding through zigzags, a broken wall and a second wall higher up. Then, turn left and continue to a junction by an orienteering marker post.

There, a path on the right rises to the nearby summit of Stott Park Heights, where a well-placed seat allows you to enjoy the splendid view in comfort. If you go to the top, return to this point to continue the walk.

8   Carry on beside the wall, now gently losing height. Eventually, the path drops through more open woodland away from the wall before reaching an obvious fork. There go left, shortly approaching a gap in a lateral wall. However, just before you reach it, turn sharp right, cross a stream and walk on to a gate. Then, bear left at the next junction and eventually pass through a gate into the access land surrounding High Dam. After joining a path from the right, the way follows the shore to the foot of the lake, which you passed at the beginning of the walk. Continue past the second pool, through a gate and down the wooded hillside beyond, retracing your outward steps to the car park.

4

Whinny Knott and Ludderburn Park

A delightful mix of forest, woodland and heathland walking, this is well saved for a fine day so that you can enjoy the expansive views it offers. Although some of the route lies along road, it is a quiet and picturesque lane – and of course, the going underfoot is easier.

Total distance: 5.6 miles (9km)
Height gain: 655 feet (200m)
Start: Pull-in by the entrance to a disused quarry, about 1¼ miles north-east of Gummers How car park.
GR.399885

1   Walk north-east along the road for 350 yards to a stile on the left, from which a path climbs into the forest signed to Blake Holme, Moor How and A592. Beyond the conifer plantation, the track continues over stiles through a more open wood, eventually turning to climb for a short distance beside a wall on the right. Past there, the way descends into denser wood, shortly dropping to a stream.

2   However, instead of crossing, turn right at a waymark to Lower Howe. Later, a stile takes you out of the wood, the path carrying on across an undulating open hillside and giving fine views beyond Windermere to a back-drop of high hills. Eventually, over a stile, the way continues beside a wall towards some buildings.

3   As you approach, bear right to follow a gated path beside them. Once past, the descent continues, leading you to a final gate/stile at the bottom from which a farm track leads across a stream to the right. Beyond that go left and walk out through a couple of gates onto a lane by The Oaks.

4   Turn right and follow the lane past the farm to a junction, about ½ mile on. Bear right towards Cartmel Fell and at the next fork, some ½

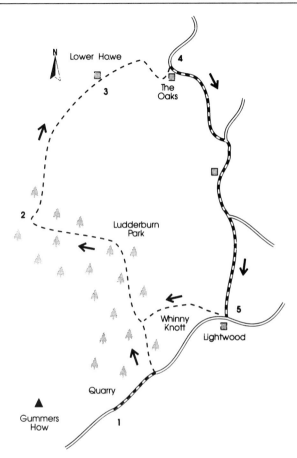

mile further, again go right. The lane affords fantastic views to the south-east before descending to a third junction by a cottage, Lightwood.

5   You can now just turn right and follow the road ¾ mile back to the starting point. Alternatively, you can leave the road through a gate on the right and climb up beside the right-hand wall. At the top corner, go over a stile just to the left and walk into the forest. A short path leads to the crossing track along which you began the walk. There, turn left and follow it back down to the road, where your car lies to the right.

5

Cartmel Fell and the Winster Valley

Beginning from the early sixteenth-century church in the tiny hamlet of Cartmel Fell, this walk explores the quiet and wooded, gently rolling hillsides that contain the course of the River Winster.

Total distance: 6.2 miles (10km)
Height gain: 655 feet (200m)
Start: St Anthony's Church at Cartmel Fell. GR.416880

1   Walk away from the church past the parish hall, turn left onto the lane at the bottom and then, at the next junction, go right. After 10 yards, follow a track on the left which leads through a farmyard and out onto another lane at the far side. Directly opposite are two field-gates, go through the right-hand one, which is signed as a footpath to Pool Bank.

2   Walk down the field, bearing away from the wall on the left to find a gated foot-bridge spanning the River Winster, part way along the bottom boundary. Across that, turn left over a gate/stile and then go right, following the field edge away from the water. Where the fence ends at the corner, carry on but bear right, guided by a waymark, to a stile in the opposite fence. Over that, a grass trod follows the edge of the pasture to a gate/stile at the far side. Now follow a fence around to the left and over another gate/stile at the top that leads into a wood. Carry on, bearing right to join a main track across a clearing, which then climbs through more trees before emerging through gates onto a lane opposite cottages at Pool Bank.

3   Turn right, walk down to a fork about ¼ mile away and bear right again to continue down the valley for about a mile. Notice, as you walk along, the names of the farms that you pass; High Low Wood, Middle Low Wood and Low Low Wood. It all becomes clear once you realise that the woodland behind is known as Low Park Wood (there is also a High Park Wood further to the west). Just beyond Low Low Wood,

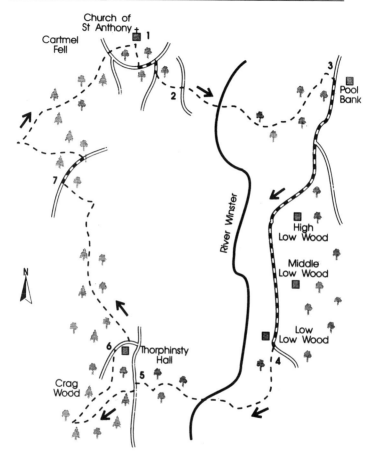

where the lane bends left, go through a gate on the right into a field, signed to Rakefoot.

4   Walk down the length of the field, following the boundary over to the right. About halfway along, where the wall ends to continue as a fence, go through a gate into the adjacent field and walk diagonally across to another gate at its far corner. Emerging onto a field track, turn right and follow it down to a gated bridge, which takes you back over the Winster. On the opposite bank, walk directly away across the field, bearing

slightly left to find a stiled foot-bridge spanning a drainage ditch on the far side. Bear right to a fence-stile near the far right corner and, over that, continue to another stile into a wood. Keep to the main path, which shortly develops as a prominent track, rising to emerge onto a lane.

5   Turn left, but after only a few yards, leave at a footpath sign through a gate on the right into Crag Wood. Follow the track for 20 yards to a bend, but there leave it at a waymark to go ahead on a faint path which climbs through bracken and, in spring, is carpeted in bluebells. Over a ladder-stile at the top, follow a fence along the edge of a plantation to another ladder-stile. However, rather than crossing, turn sharp right back on yourself to go beneath a mature oak, there is a waymark. A path then leads through the young trees to a fence-stile at the bottom. Over that, walk diagonally across to a ladder-stile in the field's opposite corner, from which a waymarked path leads left through mature woodland, eventually to leave by a gate onto a lane.

6   Turn right and walk down towards a settlement at Thorphinsty Hall. Where the lane bends right, go left onto a track beside a large house and then immediately climb a wooded bank on the left to a wall-stile. Now in a meadow beside an old barn, walk ahead following a grass trod that closes with the left boundary to ford a stream at the far end. Cross a stile into a wood and, where the path then forks 100 yards on, bear right. Further on, a ladder-stile takes the path into a field, across which yet another stile takes you back into trees. Keep going through those to a rough meadow beyond and then follow a boundary fence around a cottage garden and out through a gate in the far corner. Turn right away from the cottage, initially on a grass track and then on a tarmac drive. Shortly, after crossing a cattlegrid, go left through a gate onto a bridleway. After a brief climb, it continues through successive meadows before finally emerging onto a lane.

7   Turn right, then 200 yards along, leave through a gate on the left from which a track is signed across a bracken and tree-clad heath to Lakeside. After ¼ mile, beyond a culverted stream crossing, look for a clearing in the bracken on the right. There turn sharp right onto a path that shortly climbs to a gate. Keep going through woodland and out over a ladder-stile at the far side. With Cartmel Fell now rising to your left, walk on to another stile, beyond which the path drops over a final stile to a road junction. Cross straight over the fork to a footpath directly opposite, signed to St Anthony's Church and follow that down back to the start of the walk.

6

Staveley in Cartmel

A walk through the woods of Chapel House Plantation. Although a fair height is reached during the early stages, it is comfortably achieved along a well-graded forest track. For a few years to come, felling has revealed stunning views across the bottom end of Windermere and Newby Bridge, but in time, these will be obscured by regrowth of the forest. Railway buffs might like to wander down into Staveley in Cartmel, where there is a 7½" gauge steam railway. Although a private club, its gates are often open to the public on Sundays during the summer.

Total distance: 4.7 miles (7.5km)
Height gain: 260 feet (80m)
Start: Forestry Commission car park at Chapel House, on a minor lane south of Staveley in Cartmel. GR.381851

1   Ignoring minor paths leading off, follow a track that climbs into the forest from the small car park. Higher up, the trees that previously cloaked the hillside to the left have been felled, revealing a magnificent view across Staveley in Cartmel and the Leven Valley.

2   Beyond the clearing the climb eases and eventually, the main track makes a sharp right-hand turn. Leave it there, walking ahead on a narrower track into the trees. After about 100 yards, bear right at a waymarked fork along a twisting, undulating path. In a while, you will see a body of water through the trees to the right, Simpson Ground Reservoir. Follow the footpath to its far end, where it is joined by another path coming from below the dam. Bear left, continuing through the trees to leave the reservoir behind.

3   Keep to the main path, which eventually leads to a stone wall at the edge of the forest. There, turn right along a path that follows the wall, shortly leading across a stream. Not far beyond that point, the path leaves the wall and passes a marsh before emerging from the trees, back below the dam at Simpson Ground.

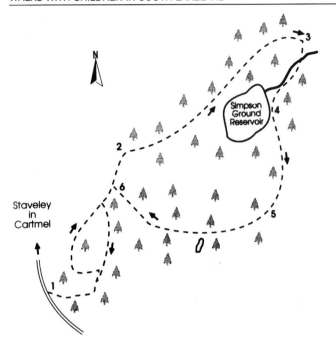

4   Turn left along a track at the foot of the dam, continuing beyond it back into the trees. A little further on, the track bends left towards a gate leading out of the forest. However, leave the track on the bend, turning right at a waymark onto a bridlepath. Where that then forks a short distance on, follow the left branch, soon to reach and then follow a wall on your left at the edge of the plantation.

5   After starting to drop, the track parts company with the wall to head back into the forest. Now more prominent, it passes small disused quarries and a tarn and is joined by a couple of waymarked footpaths from the left. Later, the track rises to a sharp right-hand bend, where you should turn left onto a rough track. After descending the forested hillside quite steeply, it emerges onto the main forest road along which you began the walk.

6   You can simply turn left and go back down the hill, however, a more interesting alternative makes use of a woodland path above the main

track. To follow this, walk down the main track for about 40 yards and then turn off left onto a waymarked path climbing into the trees. After a short pull, the path turns right at another waymark, becoming more distinct as it contours around the wooded hillside. Shortly after passing through a gap in a crossing wall, go left at a fork to walk parallel to the wall. Further on, the path begins to lose height and later leaves the wall. Now dropping more steeply, it returns to the main forest track, and the car park is then only a short distance to the left.

Staveley Model Railway

Occasionally on bank holidays and summer Sunday afternoons, the gates of the private model railway club at Staveley are open to the public. You will find it about ¾ mile away in the village, to the left of the junction at the bottom of the hill. Work is still ongoing to develop the layout, but already there is almost one mile of track, equipped with working signals, points, bridges, and a turntable; it even has its own station. Between them, the members have a number of fine steam engines, which can often be seen puffing along the line.

Commercial Forests

It was not until after World War One that many of Britain's commercial forests were first established. A prolonged blockade by the German navy had prevented vital imports from getting through, bluntly demonstrating the country's dependence upon raw materials from abroad. One particularly important commodity was timber, used amongst other things for pit props, without which the coal mines, then the nation's main source of power, could not operate. Once peace returned, many upland areas, which were otherwise unsuitable for agriculture were planted with quick growing conifers. However, the regimented plantations of single species attracted fierce criticism for being visually unattractive and incapable of supporting a varied natural flora and fauna, and as they reach maturity and are felled, more imaginative schemes incorporating a variety of different tree types are being adopted.

7

Haverthwaite to Newby Bridge

After breaking out from the southern tip of Windermere, the River Leven surges powerfully through a narrow valley between Newby Bridge and Haverthwaite. In the past, mill wheels harnessed that energy for a variety of industrial purposes including iron making, gunpowder manufacture and chemical production. All that has now passed, but some of the buildings remain and trains once again steam through the gorge, you might catch sight of them during the first sections of this walk. The return is along the neighbouring valley of Rusland, whose flat marshy floor barely rises above sea level and the river is contained behind levees to keep it on its course.

Total distance: 9.6 miles (15.5km)
Height gain: 950 feet (290m)
Start: By-lane by St Ann's Church, Haverthwaite.
GR346840

1   Walk back along the lane to the Anglers' Arms and turn right into Old Barrow Road. After 350 yards, just before a terrace of cottages, go left at a waymark beside a pair of wooden gates and drop down through a yard. Beyond the buildings, walk left through a kissing-gate and follow the ensuing riverside path to a bridge, leaving over a stile onto the road.

2   Over the bridge, turn left towards Low Wood and walk up past the former gunpowder mill and attendant cottages. Where the road then bends right, leave it for a track on the left into a wood and signed as a bridleway. At the top, it emerges from the trees through a gate, eventually leading past some houses to finish at Low Brow Edge.

3   Turn left onto a lane and walk downhill for 20 yards, crossing to a track on the right that is waymarked as a footpath. It leads past a children's play area and through a gate into an open-wooded hillside field. Walk ahead, following a fenceline to the left, soon crossing a

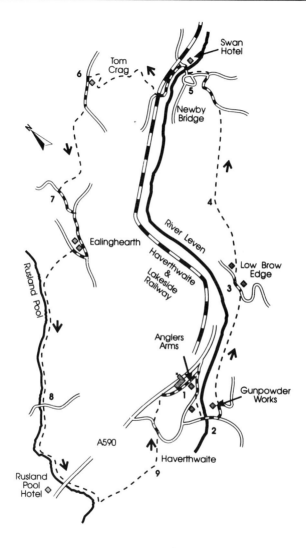

stream by a plank bridge. Further on, the fence is replaced by a wall, but continue to follow it, ignoring stiles on the left higher up. Eventually, you will reach a corner, where a ladder-stile leads ahead into the next enclosure.

4   Over that stile, bear right on an ascending grass track across open fellside. Higher up, the way becomes marshy and the track less distinct, but keep going in the same direction. Beyond the crest of the rise, walk down to join a field track coming from the right, which leads to a gate/stile in a wall ahead. Through that, a contained track winds downwards through a wood, finally ending at a lane. Turn left and walk down to the main road at Newby Bridge and go left again.

5   When you reach a roundabout junction, cross carefully to go over the bridge itself on the right and then follow the lane left in front of the Swan Hotel. Walk ahead beside the river at the junction just beyond, towards Finsthwaite and Rusland. After about 1/3 mile, the lane bends to cross the Haverthwaite Railway. Immediately over the bridge, go through a gate/stile on the right into a wood, from which a track winds upwards through the trees. At the top, where it bends sharply right, go through a double wooden gate into an open field on the left and walk away over the crest of a hill, Tom Crag, following a wall to your right. On the far side of the rise, leave through a gate on the right at the bottom and follow a farm track past some cottages to a lane beyond.

6   Follow the lane left for 250 yards to a bend, where a waymark directs you through a gate into a wood on the right. Keep to the main track, climbing over a hill and then down through successive gates on the far side, eventually emerging along the edge of the wood. You are then treated to a fine view across the Rusland valley as you continue along an enclosed track, finally leaving over a stile onto a lane where you should turn left.

7   Walk up to a junction and then go right, signed to Haverthwaite. When you reach Ealinghearth at the bottom of the hill, turn right towards Rusland, but then, after 100 yards, branch off left onto a descending track. Waymarked to Booth, it turns to follow the fringe of a coppiced wood before ending at a gate into an open pasture beyond. Carry on ahead to an embanked river and turn left to follow it downstream, eventually emerging over a stile onto a lane.

8   Go right, but then leave the lane over a stile on the left, immediately before the bridge. Continue beside the water to another road near the Rusland Pool Hotel and again cross to carry on along the riverside path.

After about ¼ mile, where the river sweeps around to the right, leave the embankment, dropping to a foot-bridge and stile leading into a field on the left. Walk to another stile opposite and continue ahead across the next pasture, following a faint track to another stile. Keep going beyond that, following the edge of a wood over to the left, eventually reaching a gate into the wood.

9   A track rises through the trees, before then dropping to a junction where you should walk left along the edge of the wood, ultimately emerging by some cottages. Go right, walk out to the main lane and there turn left. Beyond the cottages, look for a waymarked track on the right. Follow it down, choosing the kissing-gate not the field-gate, to enter a pasture over a stile at the end. Climb up the field ahead, bearing right at the top to find a gate out to a now disused lane, which leads back to St Ann's Church.

Drystone walls

Drystone walls are a common feature in the Lake District. Built without mortar, and relying for their strength on the weight of the stones, the walls often appear as ancient as the landscape across which they lie. Whilst some are truly ancient and may even be prehistoric, the majority were built during the eighteenth century, when vast swathes of the countryside were enclosed as part of a move to improve farming techniques.

Gunpowder

One of the important industries that grew up in Lakeland was the manufacture of gunpowder, a product used in vast quantities by the many quarries that operated during the eighteenth and nineteenth centuries. The surrounding woodlands provided the charcoal, and that from the juniper bush was considered to be the best, but the other essential ingredients, sulphur and saltpetre, had to be imported from elsewhere. These had to be ground to a fine powder before they were mixed in the correct proportions, and so the gunpowder mills were sited beside fast-flowing streams which could provide the necessary power. The industry declined towards the end of the nineteenth century with the development of other explosives.

8
Cartmel and Cark

*The low, wooded ridge west of Cartmel provides an enjoy-
able and picturesque route to the nearby villages of Holker
and Cark. If you want to make a full day of your excursion,
you can visit Holker Hall or, if you just fancy lunch, you will
find a pub there too.*

Total distance: 5 miles (8km)
Height gain: 425 feet (130m)
Start: Main car park in Cartmel village. GR.377787

1   Walk away from the car park across the playing field, heading north-
west to pass just left of the football and cricket pavilion. A hand-gate and
kissing-gate allow you to cross the racetrack into the woods immediately beyond. There, a track climbs a bank, before running more easily
through the trees to a squeeze-stile at the far side of the wood. Carry
on over an open rise and then down the right-hand edge of a field,
leaving through another squeeze-stile onto a lane at the bottom.

2   Turn left and follow the lane for nearly ½ mile, past Walton Hall Farm
to find a track leaving on the left, signed as a bridleway to Mount
Barnard and Hill Mill House. Follow that down, past the former mill and
beyond a gate into a wood. After climbing steadily through the trees for
about ½ mile, the track levels before beginning a gradual descent,
shortly passing out of the trees through a gate. There joined from the
right by the Cumbria Coastal Way, the track continues along the edge
of open grazing, where there is a fine view ahead across the sands of
Morecambe Bay. It ends ½ mile further on at a lane, where you should
turn right over a cattlegrid and walk down the hill.

3   Reaching a junction at the bottom, turn left and walk through Holker
village, where you pass the entrance to the Holker Estate. Carry on into
Cark, and when you reach the Rose and Crown inn, turn left beside it.
Go left again at the next junction and follow the road, which is
signposted to Cartmel and Newby Bridge, away from the village.

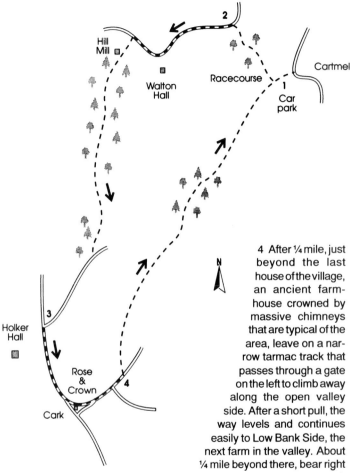

4 After ¼ mile, just beyond the last house of the village, an ancient farmhouse crowned by massive chimneys that are typical of the area, leave on a narrow tarmac track that passes through a gate on the left to climb away along the open valley side. After a short pull, the way levels and continues easily to Low Bank Side, the next farm in the valley. About ¼ mile beyond there, bear right at a junction onto a stone track, which leads down to a wood. Periodically gated, the track continues through the trees and then the fields beyond, ultimately leading you back across Cartmel Racecourse to the car park.

9

ℋampsfell from Cartmel

In contrast to the eastern wooded flanks of Hampsfell, those overlooking Cartmel are relatively open and, as the route to the top is more direct, it is thus somewhat steeper. But the climb is soon accomplished and fine views and easy walking back make it a delightful excursion. The village itself is attractive too, and it is worth spending a little time to have a look around.

Total distance: 3.7 miles (6km)
Height gain: 655 feet (200m)
Start: Main car park in Cartmel village. GR.377787

1   Walk into the village and turn right towards the priory. Go into the churchyard, past the church and then bear left to leave by a gate at the north-eastern corner onto a lane. Turn right, now walking out of the village to a junction at the end, opposite a guest house, the Glen Lea. Go left and then immediately right, climbing steps onto a footpath beside the guest house, signposted to the Hospice of Hampsfell.

● *Cartmel Priory*
● *The priory was one of several Augustinian monasteries in the North*
● *West and was founded in 1190 by William Marshall, one of Richard*
● *the Lionheart's retainers. In those days, the route to Lancaster was*
● *over the sands and the prior was responsible for maintaining a*
● *guide to lead travellers safely across the treacherous Kent estuary.*
● *At the Dissolution, the village claimed St Michael's Chapel within*
● *the priory church as its own, but the other monastic buildings fell into*
● *decay. The church we see today results from its rebuilding in 1618.*

2   Walk to a field beyond and then follow the right-hand boundary along its length towards Hampsfell, which you now see rising ahead of you. At the far end of the field, a track develops, which leads out through a gate opposite a barn. Go left but, immediately past the barn, turn right towards a kissing-gate into a field. Climb up the fields away from the farm, passing through gates at the top left hand corners until you reach

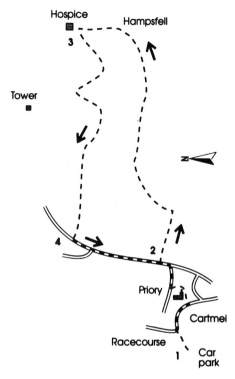

the open fellside, where a waymarked path then climbs the hawthorn and bracken-covered hill ahead. When you reach the top of the rise, turn left onto a crossing path, which now ascends more easily along the length of the ridge. Carry on where it is joined by another from the right, and later, after crossing a stile, make for the Hospice, which soon comes into view.

3　　To return, walk away from the tower, heading slightly south of west (the side of the tower carrying the steps faces approximately north), picking your way between rocky outcrops down a low escarpment onto a sloping grassy hillside. Go ahead across a grass path running at the base of the escarpment and carry on down hill. There is no obvious path, but take a line that gradually closes with a wall over to the left. Lower down, bear away from the wall to the right, where you will find a grass path, which picks through clumps of gorse, heading towards a tower, which becomes visible on the hillside, below to the north. As you approach a wall at the bottom of the fell, bear left, dropping to a gateway. Now in a field, walk down to its bottom left corner and through a kissing-gate into the field beyond. From there, a grass track continues across the fields to a farm, beyond which you will emerge onto a lane.

4　　Turn left and follow the lane for ½ mile, back into Cartmel. It will return you to your outward route at the Glen Lea, where you should then go right to walk back into the village.

10
Hampsfell from Grange

Although barely 730 feet (220m) high, the splendid isolation and positioning of Hampsfell renders it a marvellous view-point, with a magnificent panorama in every direction. In celebration of its fine qualities, the summit is embellished with an interesting viewing tower and shelter, built in the nineteenth century by Mr Remington, a one-time clergyman from Cartmel.

Total distance: 5.3 miles (8.5km)
Height gain: 900 feet (275m)
Start: Car park on the outskirts of Grange, on the B5271, just north of its junction with the B5277. GR.411783

1   From the car park turn right and walk up the lane towards Lindale. After passing Steen Heights, the last house on the left, leave the road for a footpath, signed to Routon Well and Hampsfield. A stony path climbs the wooded hillside away from the road to emerge on a tarmac drive. Cross straight over and carry on climbing through Eggerslack Wood, eventually reaching a second crossing drive higher up. Go over that as well, taking the left-hand, more prominent of the two paths opposite, signed to Hampsfell. A little higher up after bending right, the gradient eases. Keep going, ignoring lesser paths branching off, until you eventually reach a stile onto the open fell.

2   With your back to the wall, bear slightly left to climb the gently rising hillside in front of you. Before long, the route levels by a low outcrop of rock. Walk on, passing it on your right, and then make for an area of bare limestone, from which a sycamore and a couple of hawthorn bushes spring. Continue beyond those over a low ridge to join the course of a wall coming from the left. Cross it by a stile, turn right to its corner and then carry on, making for the observation tower, 'The Hospice', which marks the summit of Hampsfell.

* *The top of the tower, reached by an external staircase, has a*
* *magnificent view in all directions and is furnished with a superbly*

practical device to help identify the surrounding features. Point the revolving sighting arm to any of the distant peaks and compare the reading from its compass rose to a table at the side, which gives the bearings of everything from Blackpool Tower to Snowdon and Snaefell on the Isle of Man. For such a relatively modest climb, this must be one of the best viewpoints in the whole of the Lake District. The inside of the shelter is no less interesting, and the inscriptions around its walls provide an entertaining compensation if poor weather robs you of the view from the top.

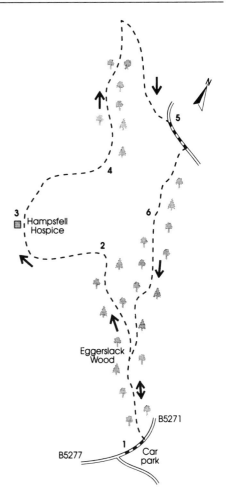

3   When you are ready to leave, walk away from the northern face of the tower (the side with the staircase), along a grass path which leads between outcrops of limestone pavement below a low escarpment on your right. Towards the far end of the escarpment, the path divides with the left fork bearing down hill. However, ignore that and carry on ahead beyond the end of

the outcrop, more gradually losing height and heading slightly east of north. After passing through a shallow depression, bear right towards a gate in a crossing wall, which leads into a wood.

4   A descending track follows the edge of a clearing, later dropping more steeply and bending to the left as it is joined by another from the right. At a fork, bear right and keep going down, eventually to reach a gate leading out of the corner of the plantation into a field. Follow the wall on your right for 25 yards to a gate/stile and cross over into a cultivated field. Turn right again, following the field edge to the corner and then go left along the boundary up the field. Carry on to a gate at a kink in the wall and cross a stile into a meadow, just to its right. Climb up, past an old lime kiln in the middle, and then bear right towards the upper of two gates at the top end of the field. Continue along a second, narrow field, which ends as a gated track into a farm. Go left as you pass the farmhouse, following a drive out to a lane.

5   Turn right, following the lane for 300 yards below a wood to some cottages, and there turn right again onto a stony track, signed as a footpath to Hampsfell. Climbing beside the trees, it leads you through a gate into a meadow, where you should continue beside the left-hand wall. Approaching its rounded corner, look for a squeeze-stile, over which a path to the right initially continues along the line of the wall before heading into trees. Where it shortly splits, take the lower path, leading to a gate and squeeze-stile, beyond which a clear descending track follows a wall on the left beside a wood.

6   A little further on, at a shallow corner, go through a gate into the wood and continue down through the trees. Where it forks just beyond a wall, keep right along the more prominent track. Lower down, after crossing a stream, again fork right and then keep to the main undulating path until eventually you join a main track from the right. Carry on down, now retracing your outward route, recrossing the two tarmac drives before you finally emerge back onto the lane. The car park then lies to the right.

11
Nichols Moss and Meathop

Barely above sea level, the land between Witherslack and the River Kent used to be tidal marshes and mud flats before it was drained for grazing. Out of its dead-flatness rise occasional rocky mounds, reminiscent of the small islands that they once were, but now surrounded by swathes of green rather than shallow estuarine waters. Meathop Fell is one of the largest of these islands and serves as an objective for this meandering countryside walk.

Total distance: 7.1 miles (11.5km)
Height gain: 195 feet (60m)
Start: By the Derby Arms north of the A590, 1 mile south-west of Millside. GR.441829

1   Follow the abandoned road south-west from the Derby Arms to the main A590. Carry on past a garage and Little Chef café and then turn right onto a gated track beside a cottage, signed as a footpath to Halecat House. After passing an overgrown lime kiln, you will emerge into the corner of a pasture. Walk ahead up the field to a stile over the fence near the top left-hand corner, which leads into woodland.

*   *To your left at that point, at the bottom of the banking, a path leads*
*   *right to a small hollow below the cliff, which was once hallowed as*
*   *a holy well. Not a well in the sense we would use today, it was a place*
*   *where water bubbled from the ground in a spring. In the pre-*
*   *Christian era, such places sometimes acquired a sacred status, the*
*   *waters being credited with curative or mystical properties, and*
*   *because the early Christian missionaries did not want to alienate*
*   *the pagan peoples, they often encouraged the wells' association*
*   *with a saint. The spring here has now all but dried up, but it is easy*
*   *to imagine the tiny cave once being used as a hermitage by one of*
*   *the early Christian aesthetics.*

2   Over the stile, walk on through a gap in the wall ahead and continue along a woodland path, ignoring any side paths. Eventually, at the far

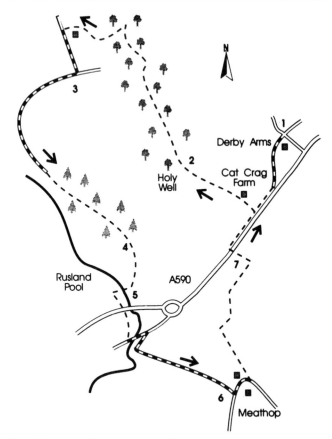

side of the wood, leave through a kissing-gate into a rough meadow. Cross that to a second kissing-gate and out onto a track towards some cottages. There turn sharp left onto a second track that leads away through trees to a stile. Now in an open pasture, turn right and walk down its length, crossing to follow the wall on the left. Approaching its far end, a path develops, which drops away right, through a shallow gully down a wooded bank. Emerging from the trees at the bottom, walk on to cross a stile and continue beside a wall past a cottage to another ŋate/stile to walk out onto a lane.

3   Go left and, at 'T' junction, follow the lane to the right, passing occasional isolated cottages. Beyond the last cottage, Dobb Coppice, the track degrades to gravel, continuing for a further ¼ mile to a fork. There, bear left on a track that is signed as a bridleway to Strip Lane, which follows a drainage ditch into the woodland of Nichols Moss. Beyond an outcrop of rock, the track emerges from the trees, passing through a gate into an open pasture, broken by rocky hillocks.

4   With your back to the gate, strike half-left to pass left of a pylon in the middle of the pasture. Go through a gate on a crossing fence and walk on to join and follow a fence over to the left. After passing a clump of trees, go through a gate on the left, turn right along a track through another gate and then cross a bridge over the River Winster. Beyond that, bend left and pass through a final gate onto a main road.

5   Take care crossing to the entrance of a field opposite and carry on ahead beside its right-hand boundary. Leave onto a lane at its far end and turn left to follow it over a bridge towards a roundabout. However, before reaching there, turn right onto another lane, signed to Meathop.

6   After about ¾ mile, at a junction below a wooded knoll and the entrance to the Woodlands Caravan site, turn left and walk up past the hamlet's few cottages. Where the lane then bends to descend the far side of the hill, turn sharp left on a footpath waymarked towards the A590. Follow it behind a cottage and between barns through a farmyard to a stile at the end of the last barn on the left. Over that, walk beside the barn and then turn right, dropping down a bank into the corner of a field. Walk away following the left-hand boundary. Cross a drainage ditch and continue to the top of the next field, there turning right to a stile in its far corner. Over that, turn right, initially following the fence on its opposite side. However, after a few yards, strike diagonally left across the width of the field, passing a marker in the middle and making for a foot-bridge in the opposite corner. Across the bridge, turn right along the field edge and, over a stile, continue along a second field. Half-way along, at a waymark, turn left and walk directly across to a stile/kissing-gate onto the main road.

7   Carefully cross to a gate opposite from which a permissive footpath avoids the road walk as far as Cat Crag. Carry on past the garage to retrace your outward steps.

12

Yewbarrow

Rising as a long wooded hill to the west of Witherslack, for very little effort, Yewbarrow's bare summit offers a splendid viewpoint over the surrounding countryside. On the way back, the walk passes Beck Head at the base of Whitbarrow, where a small river mysteriously emerges from beneath its limestone pile.

Total distance: 5.6 miles (9km)
Height gain: 525 feet (160m)
Start: By the Derby Arms north of the A590, 1 mile south-west of Millside. GR.441829

1   Walk south-west from the Derby Arms, along a lane now abandoned in favour of the adjacent A590 trunk road. After 400 yards, turn right onto a bridleway to High Fell End through the Latterbarrow Nature Reserve. Just beyond the gate, take the right fork up a wooded meadow and go ahead through another gate at the top, shortly emerging into the corner of a field. Climb away, passing left of the field's high point towards a group of cottages, which then become visible on the far side. Go through the right-most of two gates there and walk out to a lane beyond.

2   Turn left and follow it up around a bend but then, just after a garden-gate, turn off onto a bridleway on the right signed to Witherslack Hall. Follow the steadily rising track up the side of a wooded bank, going ahead where other paths cross. Higher up, the gradient eases, the trees thin out and you will shortly reach a gate/stile onto Yewbarrow's open fellside.

* *Although the path does not lead over it, the summit lies only a short*
* *distance ahead to the left. It affords a magnificent panorama that is*
* *only slightly obscured to the south by the trees through which you*
* *have climbed.*

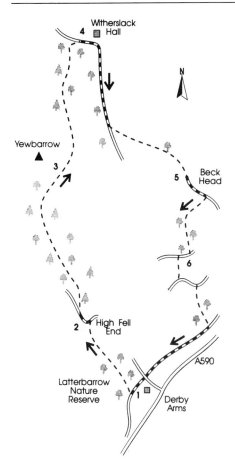

3   Our onward path from the gate lies to the right, along a clear track that falls to run beside a wall at the base of the fell. Eventually, after passing through a gate, it crosses an open field towards some cottages and then continues beyond them as an enclosed track. At a junction over a low wooded rise, go right and drop out onto a lane opposite Witherslack Hall Farm.

4   Turn right, passing the entrance to Witherslack Hall School and carry on along a quiet lane that skirts the wooded eastern flanks of Yewbarrow. After ½ mile, bear left onto a track, marked as a bridleway, which heads across the fields towards the southern end of the Whitbarrow escarpment. Through a gate beyond a wood, go ahead where the track is joined by another from the left and continue towards the cottages of Beck Head, which then come into view.

5   Carry on past a farm and, beyond it on the left, the resurgence of a stream from beneath the cliffs. Before you then reach a bridge taking the lane across the stream, turn off right onto a track. Where that then immediately forks, bear right again and follow a wall on your left

between cottages to a kissing-gate. Emerging onto a wooded heath, go ahead along a path that rises gently between gorse, bracken, bramble and hawthorn. Higher up, ignore a waymarked path off to the right and, after crossing a stream, climb to a second kissing-gate. Beyond that carry on through a wood, going forwards at another marked junction before finally leaving over a stile onto a lane.

6   Go right, but after 30 yards cross another stile on the left into a rough field, signed to Rocky Common. Walk away, bearing slightly right along a grass track that weaves between the gorse and bracken. It shortly drops into a wooded valley where it joins a small stream and then leads past a kissing-gate through which you should go out to a lane. Walk left for 100 yards to a bend and then go right along a bridleway, dropping past some cottages to emerge onto another lane a little further down. The Derby Arms lies to the right, about ½ mile away.

Cowslips

As you walk through the Latterbarrow Nature Reserve and the woodland cloaking Yewbarrow's slopes, see how many different types of wildflower you can identify. Amongst those you will spot in early spring is cowslip, readily distinguished by its several pastel yellow bell-shaped flowers, clustering at the top of a single stalk and which, with a little imagination, can be said to resemble a bunch of keys. Legend has it that when St Peter heard that a second set of keys to the Gates of Heaven had been made, he let slip his own keys, which dropped to earth and where they landed, the first cowslips sprang up.

13

Whitbarrow and Witherslack Woods

Rising steeply from the Lyth Valley, the Whitbarrow Scar culminates in an abrupt north-south ridge, which overlooks the Winster Valley to the west. Like Scout Scar above Kendal, it is formed of carboniferous limestone, and its sheer white cliffs, running for some four miles north to south, present an imposing spectacle when viewed from below. Three routes in this book explore different aspects of its character and vary the perspective of the magnificent views from the top.

Although the southern end of the ridge looks quite formidable when approached from Levens, the ascent from Mill Side follows a zig-zag route through the trees and is not overly steep. As the main climb is completed early in the walk, there is time to explore the limestone scenery along the ridge and maybe find a fossil or two.

Total distance: 6.8 miles (11km)
Height gain: 885 feet (270m)
Start: Minor lane beside the A590 at Mill Side. GR.451840

1   With your back to the main road, follow the lane towards Mill Side. After 200 yards, turn right along a track marked as a public footpath, which rises to Low Fell End Farm. Keep ahead at the top through a gate past the farmhouse and barns, beyond which are three gates. Go through the middle one, which is distinguished by a waymark and leads onto an enclosed grass and stone track. Leave through another gate at its far end into woodland, where the continuing path rises to a broad track. Turn left along it, but after 20 yards, abandon the track for a permissive path that climbs fairly steeply into the trees on the right. Ignore any side paths and follow it up, eventually reaching a small clearing where a bench invites a moment's pause to enjoy the fine view down the estuary.

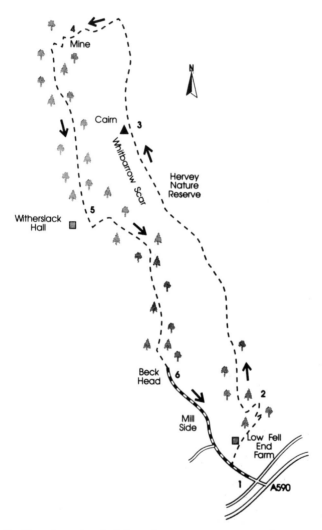

2   Now, turn sharply left, and resume your ascent of the wooded hillside. Higher up, the way crosses a broken wall and turns right, first going beside and then, a few yards on, recrossing it. With the main

climb over, the path rises more gently ahead, shortly emerging onto heath. As you gain more height, pause and look back for yet another magnificent panorama across the Kent estuary and out to Morecambe Bay. Ahead, a clear path now rises easily along a wide, undulating ridge above Whitbarrow Scar. After passing cairns marking intermediate high points, it leads to a stone wall that marks the southern boundary of the Hervey Nature Reserve. Cross a stile there and continue along the ridge until you reach the summit point, identified by a large cairn.

3   Beyond the cairn, bear right to keep to the main path, which now loses height, shortly leading to a wall. Walk on a little further, with the wall on your right, until reaching the corner of the enclosure. Ignore a stile and gate, which take the path on ahead and instead, turn left, climbing with the wall on your right. Once over the high point, the way undulates downwards towards some trees and, beneath a low outcrop of rock on your left, you will find a narrow tunnel, the entrance to an old adit.

4   After passing there, the path descends more steeply, picking its way through rocky debris to a wood below. Further down, you will pass out of the nature reserve through a gate to continue dropping through the woodland. Shortly the path levels, bringing you to a junction of paths and there, turn left onto a track, signed as a permissive footpath to Witherslack Hall. Winding pleasantly through woodland, the track leads back beneath Whitbarrow Scar. After about a third of a mile where the way divides, bear left and carry on along the main track, the route occasionally confirmed by a marker.

5   Eventually, the path emerges from the trees into a clearing below the cliffs. Walk on through a gate to reach a crossing path, there turn left and go past a football field to a gate and ladder-stile, taking you back into woodland. Ignore a track off left immediately beyond the gate and instead, continue ahead along the broad track through Witherslack Nature Reserve. After about ¾ mile, at a junction on the far edge of the wood, bear left onto a stone track that leads to a farm, at which point the way becomes a metalled lane.

6   Just past the farm, look to your left at the base of the cliffs, where an underground stream wells up from beneath the rocks. On frosty days a misty cloud smothers the resurgence, caused by water vapour, which is kept relatively warm below ground, condensing as it meets the freezing air. The lane then crosses the stream and follows it away from the settlement of Beck Head. At the end, by a telephone box, turn left, to return to the start-point of the walk.

14

Whitbarrow

Whitbarrow's eastern slopes are cloaked in forest, which, in itself, makes for an enjoyable walk. However, by climbing up to the top and then returning along the summit ridge, on a clear day you are rewarded with fantastic views across Morecambe Bay.

Total distance: 7.1 miles (11.5km)
Height gain: 950 feet (290m)
Start: Minor lane beside the A590 at Mill Side. GR.451840

1   Follow the lane away from the main road as far as the entrance to Low Fell End Farm, which lies ¼ mile along on the right and is marked as a footpath. Walk up the track and past the farmhouse and barns to three gates, just beyond them. Go through the middle one, which is waymarked, and carry on along an enclosed track, passing through a gate into a wood. Keep going to a broad track at the top and bear right.

2   Continue past the entrance to a house on the right and, where the track then bends right, itself to pass through a gateway, go ahead along a grass track, which is waymarked as a bridleway. Beyond the houses the track runs below a wooded slope, later passing into trees, where it widens and falls below former quarries. At the bottom, passing through two gates, it leaves the wood to meet a tarmac track at Raven's Lodge, where you should turn left.

3   Passing the farm, the track, which is marked as a footpath, bends right and continues beyond the quarries, eventually rising to another farm, Rawsons. Beyond a barn, turn left in front of a cottage and carry on over a stile into a wood behind. Gaining height, the way zigzags on the right, shortly joining a wall to continue the ascent. When you reach a broad forest track at the top, turn right. After 1/3 mile, in a clearing, bear left by a waymark onto a dirt track that winds into a more mixed woodland. If you reach a broad turning area, you will have just passed the junction.

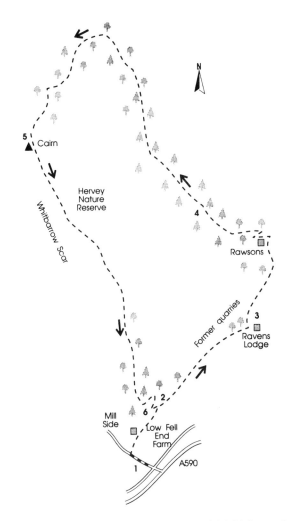

4   Occasional waymarks confirm your route, which initially, gradually gains height through the trees. Eventually the track bends and falls to a staggered junction, where you should go first right and then left,

effectively taking the route ahead. Shortly, bear right at a fork beneath a massive oak and, at the next junction where the track again splits, fork left on a narrower path. Follow this upwards for 250 yards to a cairn marking another junction and again go left. Continue upwards, eventually reaching a crossing path. There turn right and carry on to a wall, where a stile leads you out of the wood into the Whitbarrow National Nature Reserve. Over the wall go left, initially below some low cliffs, before striking off towards the higher ground, where the highest point of Whitbarrow is marked by a prominent cairn.

5   To return to Mill Side, continue ahead, following an undulating path along the broad ridge, from which there is a stunning view towards Morecambe Bay. A stile over a lateral wall takes the path out of the nature reserve, continuing beyond to the southern edge of the escarpment. There, the view disappears as you drop amongst trees, winding down to pass through a gap in a wall. After following it briefly, the path then crosses the wall again before contouring down a steep wooded bank. Eventually, when you reach a crossing path at a small clearing, turn sharp right and continue to the bottom, where the path emerges onto a broad track.

6   Turn left, but after 20 yards, leave to follow another downward path, waymarked on the right. Now retracing the steps of your outward route, leave the wood and follow the track through Low Fell End Farm and onto the road at the bottom. The main road lies to the left.

Wood anemone

Wandering through the woods in spring, look out for wood anemone, its pretty white flowers often forming areas of carpet beneath the trees. The Greek writer, Pliny, gave them the name 'windflowers' because he believe that they only opened after the wind had been blowing. Their leaves were credited with medicinal properties similar to those of the mustard plant and were gathered for use as poultices, applied to draw puss from wounds.

15

Whitbarrow from the Lyth Valley

The northern end of the ridge is less frequently visited, although it too has much to offer in its landscape and setting. This route follows the farmland fringe around its slopes before crossing the spine to return by way of the tiny hamlet of Row. The high point of the ridge lies just south of the path, and it is only a short detour to include it in the day's walk.

Total distance: 6.2 miles (10km)
Height gain: 835 feet (255m)
Start: Lay-by opposite the Lyth Valley Hotel. GR.452895

1   Immediately north of the lay-by, opposite the Lyth Valley Hotel, is an old enclosed track, climbing away from the road and marked as a bridleway. Follow it upwards to a fork in front of an overgrown ruin and bear right. Shortly joining a drive from a house over to the right, the ascent continues along the edge of a wood and ultimately ends at a junction.

2   There, turn right onto a stone track which, still rising, passes through the wood before bending around the northern end of the Whitbarrow ridge. It eventually leads through a gate into the corner of a pasture, where you should continue beside a wall on your right. The way underfoot develops as a grass track, losing height more steeply before levelling off at the edge of fields below a wooded bank. As you walk along, you have a lovely view across the Winster valley towards Cartmel Fell. A little way beyond another gate, the track bends right to drop to a lane. Although our route leaves it at this point, you might first like to follow it down to have a look at an impressive lime kiln, which stands just above the road.

3   Walk back up to the bend above the kiln and turn right onto a footpath through a gate and onwards beside a woodland fringe at the base of Whitbarrow's cliffs. After passing above a derelict farm, the path rises away from the fence, later steepening in a short pull to a wall

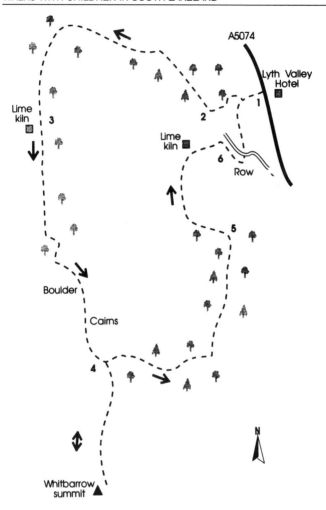

at the top. Go over a stile and then turn right along a grass path, initially beside the wall. At a corner, where it kicks off right, bear left, remaining on a faint path which then begins to rise up the hillside towards a large boulder on the skyline. Beyond there, two cairns on the horizon serve as your next markers, after which the track bears left, becoming more distinct and heading towards some trees and a lateral wall. There, go left again, follow it over the crest of the hill and then down towards a gate/ladder-stile across it.

* *You can see the top of Whitbarrow, marked by a large cairn, a little*
* *more than ½ mile away, over to the right. If you want to extend your*
* *walk to it, cross the wall here and follow the path on the other side*
* *to the top, but then come back to this point to continue the walk.*

4   Carry on down the hillside a little further, with the wall on your right to a second ladder-stile. Over that, a path leads diagonally left through the trees, and is later joined by another from the right. Continue down to the next junction at a bend, where a waymarked path leads off left. Take that and then go ahead where another path subsequently leaves on the right. After climbing through a gate, the path maintains a gradual rise between the trees, where you will find areas of limestone pavement partly hidden by undergrowth and moss. Further on the trees thin and your way is crossed by a more prominent track dropping from the left. Go straight over on a narrower path through open woodland. Keep to the main path where a lesser path then forks off left, and ignore other faint paths, which later leave on the right.

5   Shortly emerging from the wood, the way follows the edge of field enclosures, before finally ending at a gate into the corner of a field. Carry on following the right-hand wall, over which there is a wonderful view across the Lyth Valley and the little hamlet of Row, to which the circuitous path eventually leads. As you approach the houses, if you look to your left, you will see another lime kiln in the field.

6   Eventually, a gate leads out of the field into the settlement. Now on a track, walk down between the cottages to a lane at the bottom and cross over to follow a track, opposite to the left. Go left again at the end and walk away from the village. Where the track then turns right towards a house, continue ahead on a walled path, which shortly drops to a junction by the overgrown building that you passed near the beginning of the walk. Turn right and go back down to the road, taking care at the bottom, for the track emerges directly onto the carriageway.

16
Cunswick Scar

One of the finest short walks near Kendal is on to Cunswick Scar, part of a long limestone cliff that overlooks the Lyth Valley. On a clear day the views from its top into the heart of Lakeland and out to Morecambe Bay are quite stupendous.

Total distance: 3.1 miles (5km)
Height gain: 330 feet (100m)
Start: Slip road on the right, immediately north of the A591/A5284 roundabout, by the Elba Monument.
GR.496951

Elba Monument
In the field above the road at the start of the walk, rises the Elba Monument. It was erected in 1814 by James Bateman of nearby Tolson Hall to William Pitt (the Younger). Although having previously resigned as Prime Minister in 1801 over King George III's refusal to approve his Bill of emancipation for Catholics, he was persuaded back into office in 1804 by Napoleon's threat to invade England. He instituted a coalition with other European powers to overcome Bonapart's expansion of the French Empire and, following Nelson's victory at Trafalgar, became regarded as the 'Saviour of Europe'. Pitt died in 1806, but his efforts were seen as laying the groundwork for Napoleon's eventual defeat, capture and imprisonment on Elba.

Pitt's reforms of government endeared him to many of the landed gentry, including James Bateman, who conceived this monument as his own tribute to the statesman. However, Napoleon's escape in March 1815 perhaps embarrassed his gesture because the commemorative inscription he had composed was left off. It was one hundred years later that Charles Cropper, the owner of the nearby paper mill and local benefactor, finally completed the memorial by adding Bateman's intended words:

> *In honour of William Pitt*
> *The pilot that weathered the storm*
> *Elba*

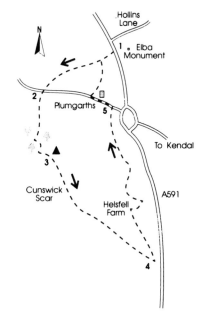

1   Walk up to the junction where Hollins Lane leaves for Burneside and, exercising caution for it is a busy road, cross over and go through a gate/stile. Walk away, heading slightly left over a rise, and dropping to a kissing-gate and drive on its far side. Go through an identical gate opposite and carry on, bearing to the right past a lone tree and then following a hedge on the left. Keep going in the same direction along the edge of the next field, emerging at its far corner onto a road. The route continues over a squeeze-stile directly opposite, signposted to Cunswick Fell and Kendal.

2   Walk to another squeeze-stile at the other side of the field, beyond which a wooded bank rises. After a further stile, a clear path works its way up through the trees, eventually levelling onto a grassy clearing where there is another stile. With most of the height now gained, the climb is less strenuous, rising easily alongside the fence on the right and over two more stiles onto the open fell above Cunswick Scar. The high point lies ahead to the left and is marked by a cairn.

3   The return route continues across the summit, maintaining the same direction. It shortly materialises as a gently descending grass track heading south-east towards Kendal, becoming visible in the valley ahead. Where the track then forks, take the left branch and keep losing height to reach a stile in the wall below. From there a green trod initially follows the wall, but then carries on beyond it, heading for a stile and bridge over the main road at the far side.

4   However, when you get there, don't leave the field, instead **turn** sharp left to walk away from the stile back across the field. Follow a line past two lone hawthorn trees and carry on to a gate in the far wall. Now follow a track down to Helsfell Farm, through the yard and out by another track at its far side. Carry on across the field, shortly leaving by a gate. Immediately beyond, climb over the fence on the left by a stile and walk away over the fields, making for an obvious white house ahead. A final stile over to its right leads out onto the road.

5   Turn left and walk up past the entrance to a self-catering complex. Just beyond that, take the next drive on the right, dropping to Plumgarth Farm. At the bottom, go right at the rear of the farmhouse and then bear left, walking away past the barns. Ahead to the right, follow a track through a gate to the fields beyond. As the field opens out, follow a grassy ridge around to a kissing-gate in the right boundary, you will remember it from the outward journey. Return to the starting point across the field on the opposite side of the drive.

Limestone

Laid down beneath a warm sea that, some 320 million years ago, covered Ireland and much of central Britain, limestone is the accumulation of fossilised shells from the creatures that once inhabited it. Look carefully at the stone and you might find fragments or even complete casts of shells, sometimes not too dissimilar from those which you can collect upon a beach, but the majority of the rock is composed of microscopic particles. Earth movements and erosion in later geological eras have removed most of the limestone that once covered Lakeland and it is now only on the fringes that isolated reefs such as Cunswick Scar and Whitbarrow remain.

17

Scout Scar

Another great favourite of Kendal's residents, this easy walk across what was once the town's racecourse onto the top of Scout Scar gives wonderful views in return for very little effort.

Total distance: 4.3 miles (7km)
Height gain: 345 feet (105m)
Start: Brigsteer Road, immediately west of the bridge over the Kendal bypass, where there is roadside parking. GR.502918

(Note that there is no access from the bypass and you should instead come from Kendal or Brigsteer)

1   Leave the road by a gated opening onto the northern end of the racecourse from which a track climbs to Bradley Field Farm. There, leave the track and carry on past the farmhouse and its attendant buildings to a kissing-gate in the top corner of the field. Keep going, following a wall on the right, climbing easily up an open, sparsely wooded heath. Where the wall later turns away, continue ahead.

2   At the top, you are led to a kissing-gate in a stone wall. Go through and continue walking in the same direction, the way rising easily to the ridge along the top of Scout Scar.

* *Many of Lakeland's placenames have their roots in old Norse words, given by the Viking settlers who came here in the tenth century. Scar or Sker means a reef or crag, and aptly describes the huge limestone cliffs that erupt in this corner of Lakeland.*

3   There is a lateral path along Scout Scar and our route back lies to the left. However, those with time and energy might first like to explore the ridge to the north. A short walk of about ½ mile along to the right will bring you to a break in the ridge that separates Scout Scar from Cunswick Scar.

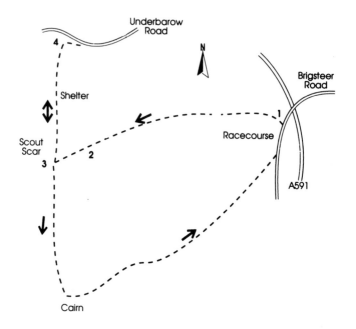

* * * * * * *
Just before there, and above the path, you will pass a circular,
domed shelter. It would, perhaps, look more at home in a British
seaside resort, but it was erected here in 1912 as a tribute to King
George V. The dome's inner rim is decorated with a, now somewhat
faded, silhouette of the skyline, identifying the principle peaks that
can be seen on a good day.

4   Go back along the ridge to the south, and after walking about ½ mile
beyond the point where you first joined it, there is a large cairn marking
a junction of paths. Turn left there and, ignoring minor crossing paths,
climb over the crest of the ridge and continue down the other side.
Eventually you will reach a stone wall that is broken by a squeeze-stile.
Beyond, a clear grassy path continues downhill and Kendal Racecourse again comes into view, the path shortly leading onto it through
a kissing-gate. Keep going across the open expanse in the same
direction to the far wall, where a stile returns you to Brigsteer Road.

18
The Hutton Villages

At one time these two villages and their surrounding hillside settlements were regarded as a single entity and the footpaths and tracks followed on this walk would have formed the daily links between the communities.

Total distance: 5.6 miles (9km)
Height gain: 540 feet (165m)
Start: Village hall by St John's Church in Old Hutton.
GR.559886

1   Leave the road along a drive lying between Old Hutton Village Hall and the C of E School, turning left behind the hall to walk over to a gate at the far corner of a grassed area. Continue in the same line over the field beyond, heading for a gate by a group of large ash trees on the far side. Through that, go through another gate on the left and turn right to climb along the field edge. Keep going over a stile at the top, dropping to a track running along the bottom of the field. Cross straight over and walk down beneath some trees to two stiles. Ignore the one on the right and climb over into a field, walking ahead beside a hedge to leave over a stream and through a gate at the far side. Carry on to a lane beyond and turn left to reach the main road.

2   Directly opposite the junction, a path leaves between two houses, crossing a stile into the field beyond. Walk on following the right-hand hedge to a waymarked stile. Over that, walk up the field beside the wall, crossing onto a green lane at the far side and turn right to return to the main road. 30 yards along to the left, leaving on the opposite side of the road, you will find a track signed to St Sunday's Beck. Go over a stile at the bottom of it and walk down a small paddock. Keep on across a marshy, uncultivated area and the field beyond, to pass through a hand-gate in the top corner. There, a foot-bridge takes you over St Sunday's Beck, the way continuing at the edge of the next field and out to a lane.

* *St Sunday is a name that crops up elsewhere in Cumbria, as in St*
* *Sunday Crag, the long ridge that runs north from Fairfield to*

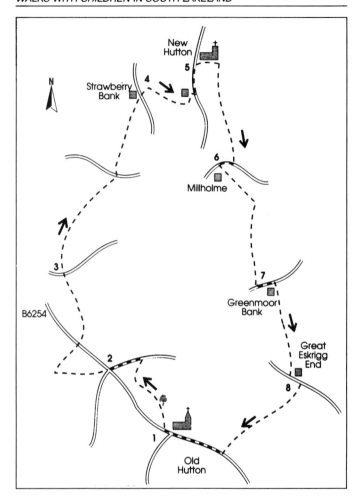

* Patterdale. There is, however, no connection between the mountain
* and the beck here, which has its source on the moors of Lambrigg
* Fell. Of St Sunday himself, there is no trace, but it is likely that the
* name is associated with St Dominic, Sunday being 'dies Dominica'
* or 'day of the Lord'.

3   Turn left, but then a few yards further on, go through a gate on the right and walk up beside the left-hand wall of the field. Over a wall-stile, continue climbing ahead in the same direction across successive fields, eventually dropping on the other side of the hill to the bottom corner of a field, where a short, walled track leads out to a narrow lane. Go up to the left looking for a gate into a field, a short way along on the right. Walk ahead across the fields, following the right-hand boundary until you eventually reach a barn at Strawberry Bank. Pass through a gate immediately before it, emerging through the farmyard onto another lane.

4   Follow the lane left for only a few yards to take a path branching right across a stream to a gate into an old orchard. However, instead of going through the gate, turn right along a narrow, walled track beside it. Beyond a low rise, it dips before climbing again, past two gates at the top to a corner. There turn left and walk around the outside of farm buildings and out on a lane at New Hutton. Turn left and walk up past the Old Parsonage to St Stephen's Church, which marks the centre of the tiny hamlet.

5   Go through the lychgate and up to the churchyard, but then immediately before the entrance gate, turn left to pass through a second gate onto a track. Walk right, following the track around the back of the church, and then go through the second field gate on the left. In the field, walk diagonally right, passing behind the former school to a stile and maintaining your direction across successive fields until a final stile leads out onto a narrow enclosed path. Follow it left to the bottom, where it emerges onto a lane at Millholme.

* *Impressively adorning the tops of gate pillars by St Stephen's*
* *Church are two greyhounds, which were the symbol of the Sleddall*
* *family and originally decorated the entrance to their estate before*
* *the mansion was demolished in the latter part of the nineteenth*
* *century. Thomas Sleddall, a lawyer, was the first mayor of Kendal*
* *in 1636 and his descendants were wine merchants in the town,*
* *founding a school and building almshouses there.*

6   Walk along the lane to the right as far as a white house and turn down the second of two tracks on the left to pass beside it. Over a beck and through a gate at the bottom, turn right and walk up through a farm to three gates. Go through the one on the right and into the corner of a large rising pasture. Strike half-left to climb up it over a hill to a ladder-

stile beyond its crest. Across that, bear right, heading towards a house now visible in the middle distance, where you cross out onto a lane.

7   Go left to Greenmoor Bank Farm and immediately after the house, turn right into the farm. Walk through the yard, leaving by a gate directly ahead at its far side into a field and carry on, beside a hedge on your right to a foot-bridge at its far side. Over it, climb the next field passing right of a pylon and on over a crossing track at the top to the far corner, where a plank bridge leads through a hedge into another field. Carry on down and out through the gate and yard at the bottom onto a lane at Great Eskrigg End.

8   Just to the left is Little Eskrigg End Farm, through which a sign directs you right to Bridge End. Leave the farmyard by a gate opening just to the right of a barn and climb up the right-hand hedge of a field, crossing a fence towards the top. Keep the same direction across subsequent fields, crossing first a stile and then passing through a gate. Beyond the gate, bear right down towards a clump of trees, beyond which a gate takes the way through to the next field. Walk on down beside the left boundary and out through a gate at the bottom onto a track. Turn left to reach the road and then follow it to the right, back into Old Hutton.

* *Old Hutton*
* *John Wesley, the founder of Methodism, spent much of his life*
* *travelling the length and breadth of the country, preaching sermons*
* *and distributing charity amongst working class families. It was*
* *during such a journey, from Whitehaven to Leeds, that on the 3*
* *October 1794, he passed through Old Hutton, taking lodgings at the*
* *cottage opposite St John's Church. St John's itself is an attractive*
* *and well proportioned structure, built in 1873 to replace an earlier*
* *church that existed on the site. It is generally open and inside you*
* *will see that, although electric lighting is now installed, the original*
* *oil lamps still hang from the roof.*

19

Along the Lancaster Canal

After roaming out over open fields, this walk joins the Lancaster Canal on its sinuous route south of Kendal, weaving across the rolling countryside in search of a level course towards the town. One of the walk's interesting features is the Hincaster tunnel, dug straight through a hill to avoid what would otherwise have been a considerable detour.

Total distance: 5.9 miles (9.5km)
Height gain: 490 feet (150m)
Start: Minor road north from Hincaster, immediately south of a bridge taking it over the A590 where there is room to park off the road. GR.506862

1   Follow the lane over the main road and immediately beyond, climb a banking on the right into a rising field. Walk ahead, initially beside the right-hand fence and continuing beyond it to a lone bridge, which once spanned the canal. Cross it from the left and, once through a gate, walk away across the pasture towards a clump of trees towards its far side. Climb beyond the trees to an indented field corner, where there is a thoughtfully placed seat, and down the other side of the hill to a gate onto Well Heads Lane.

2   Cross to a stile, just to the right and follow the right-hand hedge over the hill in front to a stile by a railway line at the bottom of the next field. There, a detour and footbridge take the way across the track into the field opposite. Walk over to a stile part way along its left-hand boundary and then keep the same north-easterly direction over subsequent fields, heading towards some trees and a building, Crosscrake Primary School, which come into view ahead.

3   Emerging onto a lane beside the school, turn left, but after a few yards, pass through a gate on the right and walk across a field to a gate/ stile in the far right corner. Now, climb beside the wall on the left up the

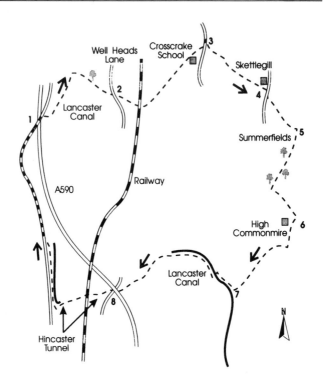

next couple of fields to the top of the hill, continuing ahead, steeply down its opposite side to a gated bridge into Skettlegill Farm, which you will then see at the bottom. Walk through the farmyard to the right to reach the lane beyond.

4   Go through a gate on the opposite side of the lane and walk up beside a building to a gate ahead (ignore one on the right). Carry on to a stile in the hedge on the skyline and keep the same direction across the next field to another stile in its far corner. Over that, walk directly ahead across the field to its far wall and then go right to a stile, leading out onto a track near Summerfields.

5   Follow the track right, passing the base of a ruined lime kiln in the bank on the right, and on through a kissing-gate. Keep going beside a

small wood and then ahead, where the track broadens into a meadow to reach the furthest of two gates on its opposite side. A path continues through a narrow wood, shortly leading to a stile in a wall on the left, just before a field gate. Cross into the field and head directly over to a gate on its far side and through that, turn right along a track to High Commonmire Farm.

6   Go through the farmyard to pick up the continuation of the track and when you shortly reach a junction, turn right following a narrow lane down through the fields to the Lancaster Canal. At a bend, just below the canal embankment, leave the track and climb up to the canal, the way signed to Well Heads Bridge and Stainton.

7   Turn right along the canal and, at the next bridge, cross over to continue in the same direction on the opposite bank. Notice, a little further on, that the canal is carried above a stream on an aqueduct. Beyond the next bridge, the canal has been filled in, but the towpath remains obvious and continues beneath another bridge, eventually emerging through a gate onto a lane. Turn left and follow it beneath a road bridge and then, immediately beyond, go through a gate on the right into a picnic area. Here, the canal reappears, running into a deepening cutting and the entrance to the Hincaster Tunnel. There is a wooden observation platform in front of the portal, which gives you a good view right through.

8   There being no towpath through the tunnel, you must now follow the path that the horses took, which climbs above the cutting on the left and over the top of the hill. On the far side, just before you reach a lane, turn right to go behind a cottage and rejoin the canal. Where you are forced back onto the lane a third of a mile further on, keep going to return to your car.

20
Sizergh Castle and
Helsington Church

For those with an interest in ancient buildings, this walk has the added interest of linking Levens Hall and Sizergh Castle. Each was originally built as a stark pele tower, but as life became less violent, they evolved into the more extravagant buildings we see today. Beyond Sizergh, the way leads on to the eighteenth-century St John's Church at Helsington and then back through the delightful Brigsteer Wood.

Total distance: 7.5 miles (12km)
Height gain: 690 feet (210m)
Start: Lay-by beside the A6, immediately north of Levens Bridge. GR.496852

1   Walk towards the bridge, but before crossing, go through a gate on the left into Levens Park on the northern bank of the river. From there, a waymarked path leads on through the park.

2   At the top end, go out of the park into a field and follow its boundary wall to the right. Keep ahead across the next field towards cottages at Park Head, where you emerge onto a lane. Turn left and walk to the main road at its end.

3   Go straight over and follow the continuing lane, past Heaves Hotel to a junction. There, turn left onto a track towards Heaves Farm, bearing right where it almost immediately forks, to rise along a wooded bank to Wayn Gap Cottage. Continue through a kissing-gate beyond the cottage and keep ahead alongside fields until you reach the farm. Carry on into the yard and then turn right to a lane.

4   Cross a stile directly opposite, signed Sizergh Castle, and walk away over a rough pasture, heading half-right towards the corner of a wood and a gate into the adjacent field. Carry on, now bearing left,

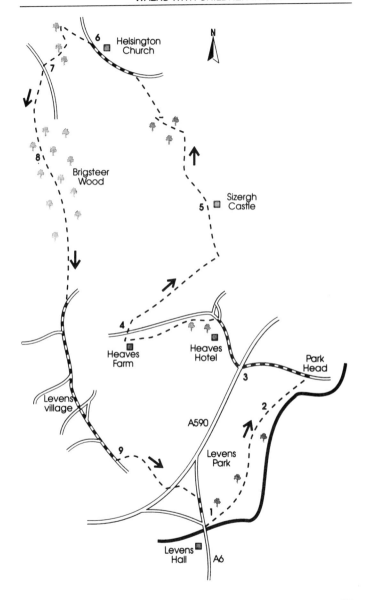

climbing over the rise of the field to find a gate part-way along its left edge. Continue in the same direction across the subsequent field, dropping to kissing-gates in its far corner. Go through the one in the wall on the left and walk ahead along the field edge to reach a car park at Sizergh Castle.

5   Walk through the car park to a drive leading from the castle, and cross over to a field-gate opposite. From there a footpath, signed to Helsington Church, heads across the field to a gated opening in its far corner. Then carry on along a gravel track, which rises towards a barn in the middle distance. There, go left to a stile and on along a path through a narrow strip of woodland. Rejoining the track at the top, turn right and walk down to a gate into a field on the left. Through that, walk up on a sharp left diagonal to a stile and maintain the same direction across the next field. You will eventually join a metalled track coming from the right leading to Helsington Church, which soon comes into view ahead.

6   Just beyond the church, opposite a building that was once its school, bear left down a grassy slope, dropping to a stile into woodland at the bottom. The ensuing path continues down through the trees, ending at a broad track. Turn left and take the left branch when it then forks, walking beyond a cottage to a gate at its end. Go right, down to a field, and then continue to the bottom, leaving through a gate by some barns onto a lane.

7   Cross over into the field opposite and walk to its far bottom corner, where a gate leads into Brigsteer Wood.

8   At the first fork, bear right and then keep going ahead, eventually emerging from the wood at its far side onto a track. Go left, walking to its end and then turn right onto a lane, following it into Levens village. Keep to the main street, going ahead at a crossroads by the Methodist Church and walk on, soon to pass a small housing estate on the left.

9   Towards the end of the houses, turn left along a drive to 'Ringing Stones', signed as a footpath to Levens Bridge, and continue into a field at the bottom. Cross to a ladder-stile and carry on, finally leaving the fields on a track, which takes you over a bridge and eventually back to the road, just north of Levens Bridge.